As you set out to master the art of eff  ɔ in mind that the first rule of pitching is to ʾhat is your elevator pitch? An experienced b ːhes are the ones that can be summed up in one compelling sentence.

What one sentence best captures the essence of your company?

Let's dissect it even more. This book aims to provide you with tried-and-true tactics that will turn your pitch from mediocre to outstanding. Every chapter reveals crucial methods, such as developing an engaging story, comprehending the psychology of your audience, honing your delivery, and using storytelling as an effective tool. These aren't simply theories; they're tried-and-true strategies that have assisted business owners in thriving in cutthroat environments.

Think about the impact of a strategic question. Many times, in the rush of pitching, people forget to be explicit about their goals. When it's time to wrap up your pitch, make sure you make your request with assurance. Are you trying to find an investment? Collaboration? A guide? Give it a proper spelling. It's the distinction between a specific call to action and an ambiguous suggestion.

IMAGINE FOR A MOMENT that you have humanised your pitch. You begin with a human story before delving into the unique product's technical specifications. You remember that turning point in your life when you realised your company was solving a very personal issue. Maybe the day you witnessed a loved one suffer because there were no green energy options available to them inspired you to turn waste plastic into biodiesel. All of a sudden, your audience is experiencing your enthusiasm and intensity directly rather than just listening to your pitch.

You'll learn the value of authenticity in your storytelling throughout this book. Stakeholders of today are astute; they can detect dishonesty immediately. Thus, when pitching, present your genuine self to the audience rather than just reading from a script. Talk about your setbacks, your victories, and the unfiltered feelings that keep your passion of entrepreneurship alive. Your audience will relate to you and your cause more if you are willing to be vulnerable.

BUT LET'S NOT FORGET about the technical side of pitching. It takes hard planning and consideration to create a captivating presentation. Your pitch's organisation is just as important as its content. This book will teach you how to create a pitch that guides your audience through the lifecycle of your company in a smooth and coherent manner. We'll look at how to strike a balance between facts and feelings, demonstrating how well-researched facts may support engaging tales without giving your audience too much information.

Practice does, after all, make perfect. You get more accustomed to the process the more pitches you make. Additionally, each pitch presents a distinct chance for development. It involves honing your message, modifying your delivery, and developing the ability to gauge the responses of your audience. Every experience broadens your skill set and increases your versatility and self-assurance as a communicator.

GET READY TO APPRECIATE the response art. After every pitch, ask for helpful feedback. What struck a chord? What gave way? Maintain the cycle of improvement by using this priceless input to improve your abilities. Never forget that even seasoned business owners are always learning and evolving, so seize the chance to advance.

As we delve deeper into the book's chapters, you'll come across actual case studies from business owners who have experienced what you're about to go through.

Their achievements and setbacks supply you knowledge about what functions well and poorly, assisting you in navigating the subtleties of creating a pitch that genuinely stands out.

Pitching is dynamic; there is a new context for every audience, every room, and every moment. That's what makes it so beautiful. The best ally you have is adaptability. While some investors might be convinced by an emotive story, others might prefer objective evidence.

You can make your pitch more effective by knowing your audience and what they require.

Are you prepared to take centre stage now? Are you ready to turn your company concepts into an engaging story that has an enduring effect? Here are

How to
Pitch
Your
Business

Proven Strategies
To Stand Out
and Win Over
Stakeholders

JOSHUA ZAGHE

How to Pitch Your Business: Proven Strategies to Stand Out and Win Over Stakeholders

JOSHUA ZAGHE

Published by BILLY GRANT, 2024.

HOW TO PITCH YOUR BUSINESS: PROVEN STRATEGIES TO STAND OUT AND WIN OVER STAKEHOLDERS

First edition. October 7, 2024.

Copyright © 2024 JOSHUA ZAGHE.

ISBN: 979-8227331977

Written by JOSHUA ZAGHE.

Also by JOSHUA ZAGHE

Table of Contents

*To my mentor **Vusi Thembekwayo.***

INTRODUCTION

BEING SEEN IS MORE than simply a goal in the hectic world of enterprise. Imagine this: You enter a room full with possible partners, investors, and influencers, each of them a crucial step towards the success of your company. Opportunities abound, but there is intense competition. How can you ensure that your voice is heard above background noise?

How can you take your ideas and turn them from empty concepts into gripping stories that move others to action?

Introducing the art and science of business pitching, a crucial talent that could determine the success or failure of your entrepreneurial endeavours. It takes more than just quoting data and facts to engage an audience; you also need to tell a compelling story that entices them to follow you on your trip.

EVERY PROSPEROUS BUSINESSPERSON is aware that every pitch requires a deeper comprehension of not just what they are selling but also why it is important. It all comes down to stating the issue you are trying to solve and why your solution is the best one. For a brief moment, picture yourself in the crowd, listening to different pitches. What remains? What got someone to that very moment—the impassioned story of a journey, or the dry statistics?

INDEED, THE THINGS that leave a lasting impact are the anecdotes, the intimate touches, and the related experiences.

As soon as you enter that imaginary stage, you need to draw attention to yourself. Your intensity, tone, and body language all have a significant impact on how your pitch is received. All too frequently, business owners hide behind their PowerPoint slides and expect the slides to speak for them. However, let's face it: the storyteller is what people remember, not the slides.

When was the last time you were enthralled with a speaker? What made them stand out in your opinion? They captivated their listeners, met their eyes, and enthusiastically expressed their passion.

tried-and-true techniques that will help you become an effective pitch presenter and help you stand out from the competition. Take a deep breath, absorb the teachings, and observe how your company not only becomes the envy of stakeholders but also gains their unwavering trust.

CHAPTER 1

UNDERSTANDING THE POWER OF A PITCH

There is more to a pitch than just a presentation. It's a chance to show others what you perceive and lead them on a trip that will ultimately lead to success for you and your stakeholders. Your pitch has the ability to persuade listeners to believe in your idea, change their opinions, and open doors.

HOWEVER, IT INVOLVES more than just reciting information while standing in front of an audience. It's an opportunity to capture, elicit strong feelings, and spur action. If you do this well, your pitch can become a potent instrument that shapes the direction of your company.

So, how can you arouse empathy? Begin by being aware of your opponents. Most are, your audience has heard hundreds or maybe thousands of pitches. Buzzwords and general statistics have no effect on them.

They're taught to tune out the distractions and concentrate on the important stuff. The key to a great pitch is standing out in a way that feels true, genuine, and confident. This does not require you to instantly come up with a game-changing concept, but it does require you to be aware of the subtleties of connection and persuasion.

The psychology of the pitch is one item that cannot be disregarded. It's essential to read the room, understand your audience, and address their needs instead of your own.

Customers, partners, and investors all have different goals and interests. What drives them? Is there a monetary reward? An opportunity to join something greater? Is it the straightforward assurance that a problem they've been battling for a while would be resolved? Using those unadulterated human emotions and incorporating them into your story is where a pitch's strength resides.

Imagine yourself on the other side of this now.

YOU'RE SITTING IN A room full of decision-makers who've seen a hundred other entrepreneurs that week. What would draw your interest? It's unlikely to consist solely of data or a well-designed PowerPoint. It will be the tale that stays with you, one that resonates, provokes thought, and even evokes emotion. The best pitches leave a lasting impression in addition to being informative. They give stakeholders the impression that they are joining a mission rather than merely making an investment.

WHEN WAS THE LAST TIME a speaker actually moved you? It probably wasn't because they were technically perfect. It was a result of their actuality. You were moved deeply by their words since they were delivered with conviction and emotion. That's what your pitch must do. Put aside the jargon and your attempt to sound impressive, and just concentrate on being a human. Talk to the people in your audience like you would a friend. Make them understand the reasons behind your intense passion for what you do.

The true magic happens right here. Being passionate is not enough; you also need to organise your pitch to keep the audience's interest and generate momentum. Consider your pitch to be an exhilarating experience. There are quiet passages when you're establishing the scene, followed by sharp ascents where you create suspense, and lastly, the thrilling descent where you unveil your game-changing concept or demand action. Your pitch should flow naturally yet with a purpose.

IN ORDER FOR YOUR AUDIENCE to be not just persuaded but also eager to move forward after you're done, you want to lead them through the highs and lows of their emotions.

In this equation, telling stories turns into a crucial component. People are story-responsive by nature. They are our means of processing information, connecting with one another, and making sense of the world. Incorporating a narrative into your pitch provides your audience with a concrete hook, making it memorable and relatable.

Saying your product will address a problem is one thing, but demonstrating it with a real-world example of someone who has encountered the issue and how your solution improved their life is quite another. This is when a pitch's strength really shines—not in the statistics, but in the intimate bond you establish with the audience through your narrative.

To be clear, however, telling a story does not imply straying from the facts. Data has a role, but it needs to be strategically used.

Select the data that will have the greatest impact on your audience rather than boring them with endless numbers. What are the figures that tell the most compelling version of your story? Suddenly, that 10% statistic is more than just a number; it's a relatable benefit your audience can grasp. For instance, instead of saying, "Our product increases efficiency by 10%," paint a vivid picture: "Imagine saving 4 hours a week—hours you could use to grow your business, spend time with family, or invest in new opportunities."

Learning how to deliver things well is another component of the puzzle. Even the most well-structured pitch can fall flat if it's presented with poor energy or a lack of conviction. It matters as much that you are in the room as that you say things. Maintain eye contact, project authority with your body language, and remain enthusiastic during the pitch. Your audience will look to you for guidance. They will be able to sense your excitement. Your nervousness or uncertainty will transfer to others as well.

TO ACE YOUR PITCH, you don't need to be an extrovert; all you need to do is practise stating your points with conviction.

There's also the issue of timing. Excellent pitches are brief. Without wasting time, you must say what needs to be said. Consider the time of your audience. Since they are busy individuals, they will value your ability to get right to the point. This doesn't imply you rush through your presentation, but rather that you focus on the fundamentals and leave out everything that doesn't advance the conversation ahead.

Consider your pitch as a teaser rather than the entire movie. You're providing just enough information to pique the attention of and want for more from your readers.

Naturally, each pitch has its own rhythm, so flexibility is key. Not every moment will afford you the luxury of a formal presentation. Sometimes, your pitch could be impromptu—at a networking event or in an elevator with a possible investor. You must be prepared to modify your strategy in response to changing circumstances.

The most skilled pitchers are those who can change direction quickly and adjust their message to suit the situation. It's this quick thinking that makes outstanding pitchers stand out from the rest.

It's also important to keep in mind that a pitch is a two-way conversation. It's important to listen as well as present. Keep an eye on how your audience responds. Do they concur by nodding? Do they look confused? In real time, modify your pitch according to the cues you discern.

The Psychology of Persuasion

When used skilfully, persuasion can change the course of events, expand on previously unimagined possibilities, and captivate individuals without them realising it. The secret to persuasion is striking a balance between logic and emotion, two strong factors that, when combined, may make nearly any argument persuasive. But you can't pull mechanical levers to control these forces.

THEY'RE WOVEN INTO the fabric of human decision-making, guiding thoughts, feelings, and actions, often without even being observed.

Appealing to emotions immediately appeals to the heart. Bypassing logical thought processes, they elicit strong emotional responses, recollections, and firsthand experiences from the listener. When was the last time you were convinced to act on your feelings rather than on objective, factual information?

EMOTIONS FREQUENTLY have a stronger hold on us than we would like to acknowledge, whether it was purchasing a product because the brand made you feel important or contributing to a cause because it matched your basic principles.

In business, the same rules apply. Stakeholders—whether they're investors, clients, or partners—are still human. Pitch that piques their interest draws them in. This doesn't imply they'll ignore reason, but if you can appeal to their feelings, you've already made a significant initial move in their direction. It can be the thrill of being a part of something fresh and inventive, or it might be the consolation of knowing they're funding a project with a strong moral foundation. Knowing which emotions are most important to your audience will help you target any emotion.

Here's where logic comes in—the other side of the equation. Your pitch will be grounded in facts, figures, and logical reasoning, which will give it weight and authority. Emotional appeals can hook your audience, but reasoning reassures them that they're making a solid decision. Making someone enthusiastic about your idea is one thing, but they also need to have faith in its potential for success. Logical appeals, then, aren't about bombarding your audience with information. They centre on the strategic application of statistics to support your arguments. What will have the biggest influence? Is the statistic timely? A market trend that's hard to overlook? Or maybe it's a clear financial prediction that displays indisputable potential?

PERSUASION BECOMES effective when it strikes a balance between rational and emotional arguments. If you show too much emotion, you run the danger of coming across as unrealistic or unfounded. If you use too much reasoning, you risk coming out as aloof or disengaged. The intersection where both components work well together is known as the sweet spot. Your pitch should satiate the intellect as well as the soul.

BUT HOW DO YOU PUT emotion and logic together in a way that sticks with people? Here's when narrative becomes important. For millennia, people have used stories to impart knowledge, morals, and beliefs. They make a world that people can inhabit, which makes them unforgettable. Telling a tale allows you to do more than just impart knowledge; it allows the listener to put themselves in the story.

Think about this: describe how your business idea came to be rather than just listing its features and benefits in a list of bullet points.

What trouble were you facing? In what way did the answer become apparent to you? More significantly, after this answer is put into practice, what will the future hold? All of a sudden, you're telling a story instead of just making a presentation. And your stakeholders are part of that story. They no longer just listen passively; instead, they participate in the success and resolution of the story.

Storytelling's versatility is what makes it so beautiful. Your story can be tailored to your audience's particular values and requirements.

Perhaps the storyline for investors revolves around market demand and development possibilities. Perhaps the most important thing to customers is the human impact—how your good or service improves people's lives. You may make sure that the facts and numbers are absorbed organically rather than as a distinct, stand-alone component of the pitch by weaving your logic into the narrative.

A COMPELLING NARRATIVE transcends the facts. It has the ability to change people's viewpoints and elicit empathy in previously unresponsive ways. However, it's crucial to keep in mind that the narrative must be true. Audiences nowadays are able to detect oddities. They quickly discount stories that appear contrived or deceptive. Finding your story's real core—the reason for your actions—and presenting it in a way that appeals to the values of your audience are the keys to success.

It's not the purpose of captivating stakeholders with flowery language or excessively intricate slideshows. Making them experience something genuine is the goal. And once they sense it, reason will support their choice. They will proceed not because they have been duped but rather because they sincerely think your idea will work.

Knowing people entails knowing the psychology of persuasion. What motivates them? What concerns them? What moves them to take action?

Logic and feelings are merely means to an end—a means of bridging the distance between your idea and their readiness to support it. However, when used effectively—through the narrative power—they don't just affect decisions; they change them.

One of the most difficult things about pitching is always having to strike a balance between logic, emotional appeal, and storytelling. Far too many individuals believe that having a fantastic product or service is sufficient.

The Anatomy of a Successful Pitch

Building a bridge between where you are and where you want to take your audience is analogous to crafting the ideal pitch. It's not just a speech or a set of slides; rather, it's a flow of well crafted elements that, when put together harmoniously, have the ability to lead stakeholders from a state of early inquiry to complete commitment. Even though a pitch seems flawless in its execution, every pitch has an underlying structure that keeps it together.

Understanding the structure of an effective pitch—that is, what makes it compelling enough to compel listeners to take action—is essential to crafting anything effective.

Let's first discuss the issue. It's not just an opening phrase that should identify the problem; it's the hook. Making your audience feel the weight of the issue you're addressing is the first step in drawing them into the story you're about to tell. It goes beyond just expressing the obvious. Making the problem accessible, concrete, and real is key. For an investor, it's the missed chance in the market. It's the regular pain spots that a client experiences. Your objective is to describe the issue in a way that makes the people in the audience nod in agreement, as though you are addressing their grievances directly. You want them to experience the pain that only your remedy can relieve.

Correctly solving the problem requires more than just having reliable information. It all comes down to how you frame the problem. Perhaps the issue is one that, until you put it in perspective, they were unaware even existed.

The key is to make it vivid—paint a picture of what's at risk rather than merely describing it. Give examples, tell tales, and help people see the rippling affects of this problem being left unaddressed. It all comes down to telling a story that enables them to visualise the outcomes in the actual world. You're not fixing any problems at this point. You're building suspense and laying the groundwork for your answer, the protagonist of the tale.

DON'T RUSH ENTERING the solution. It has to be developed. The answer should seem like the final piece of a puzzle that your audience was working on without even realising it. This is your moment to shine and show off how brilliant your concept is. But keep in mind that offering a solution is more than just listing features. It's about demonstrating why this is the best potential solution and how it directly addresses the issue you just described.

YOUR ANSWER MUST SEEM obvious and like the most reasonable way to wrap up the tale you've begun. And yet, it should still have that spark of novelty, something that makes the audience lean in because they can sense the opportunity in it. The important thing is to demonstrate that this is more than just a concept on paper, whether that is done with statistics, a case study, or a real-world example of your product. It's real, it's palpable, and it works.

USING THE PROCESS OF discovery to guide your audience is one of the best methods to accomplish this. Show them how your solution fits into their reality, how it operates step-by-step, and why it is ideal for the problem at hand. Not only are you providing a solution, but you're also leading them to believe that this is the only feasible one.

Remember to illustrate the value as well. What changes will this solution bring about? What constitutes success, and how will it alter the lives of those who matter most to you?

You're offering a vision for the future in addition to just solving a problem. Verify that their view of it is as clear as yours.

Now comes the bit that typically gets skimmed over: the ask. Without a direct and unambiguous call to action, the pitch's structure is lacking. Pitch, after all, is never formed in a vacuum. You are there in order to obtain finance, authorisation, a partnership, or a contract. But if you're not careful, this is where things can spiral out of control.

HOWEVER COMPELLING the problem or solution may be, your pitch will fall flat if the ask is poor or ambiguous.

It's a question of confidence and clarity. You must be very clear about what you want, why you want it, and how much it will cost them. Too frequently, people are scared to ask for too much, but underselling oneself might make your audience question your conviction. You are encouraging the stakeholder to participate in the narrative you have just given when you make the request.

They are more than simply spectators; they are part of the process of realising this goal. Since the goal is ultimately to create a shared future, your ask—whether it be for money, resources, or support—should be as thrilling as your answer.

Don't make the request the last one in order for this to succeed. Problem, solution, ask—this is how a pitch should go naturally. The foundation is in place by the time you reach this point. The ask should feel like the appropriate thing to do if you've done it correctly.

More significantly, it seems to be beneficial to both parties.

The request goes beyond the simple business at hand. It has to do with letting someone into a relationship. You're offering them the chance to join you in this venture, to be part of something bigger. But it's vital that you're specific. Declare your requirement for $1 million in funding. Make it clear whether you want them to sign a cooperation agreement. It is easier for them to behave if you are more direct with them. Make sure they don't wonder what will happen next.

The ability to organise these fundamental components effectively determines the structure of a pitch. A excellent pitch, even with just one speaker, is a dialogue rather than a monologue. Because of how inherently the problem, solution, and question fit together, you are steering the audience through a process that will ultimately lead them to a decision that feels inevitable.

CHAPTER 2
CRAFTING YOUR BUSINESS NARRATIVE

All businesses have a narrative, but the secret is to create one that profoundly connects with the target audience. Your story isn't just a dry historical overview or a dry facts list. It's a chance to influence perspective, arouse belief, and forge a bond that goes beyond standard business conversation. A well-crafted story takes what can seem like mundane events and turns them into a riveting journey, full of suspense, struggles, and, finally, successes. This has nothing to do with embellishing or oversimplifying; rather, it's about identifying the essential emotion that drives your company.

It starts with the individuals that run the company. Why should anyone care who they are? A good story pulls back the curtain and reveals the characters, the passions, and the drive that carried this idea forward. Perhaps an epiphany came from a frustrated moment, or maybe it all began in a garage.

Perhaps the vision started out as a way to solve an issue that nobody else could see. These are not only insignificant features; rather, they represent the foundation of something far more significant.

Upon starting to compose your business narrative, it is imperative that you consider the "why" behind your company's existence. What propels it ahead? Corporate speak should not obscure the answer to that query. It must have a genuine, human, and raw feeling.

Every company has a goal, and you'll be well on your way if you can express that goal in a way that appeals to the interests and concerns of your target audience. Instead of merely believing in what you're selling, you want them to believe in who you are.

But there is more to your tale than your origins. It concerns your destination. There should be forward momentum in your story. It's the story of your beginnings, to be sure, but it's also the story of your future.

PEOPLE WANT TO FEEL as though they are joining a rapidly expanding enterprise while they are listening to a business story. Something living, something changing. Your narrative should develop momentum by making references to the future you're creating and its potential effects.

Storytelling in business often involves embracing hurdles, the friction that makes your path compelling. It isn't relatable or credible to hear about easy sailing from the beginning, so nobody wants to hear that.

You have to mention challenges, hardships, and moments of uncertainty in your story. These provide your company a more relatable and honest feel that audiences are drawn to. These vulnerable moments, whether they be from the early days of bootstrapping, a near-miss failure, or a daring risk that paid off, are what give your story authenticity.

But what use is a task if it remains unsolved? Every story has to have a pivotal moment—the point at which things started to get better, when all of the effort paid off, or when a crucial choice changed the direction of the company. This is where you present the fix, the lightbulb that turned the issue into advancement. This is your company's lifeblood, the concept that served as the basis for everything else. At this point, your audience begins to see not only the knowledge and strategic acumen that have propelled your company's success, but also the passion that lies at its core.

The way you organise the tale is equally crucial to crafting a compelling business narrative.

It is a narrative arc, in which each episode builds upon the one before it, rather than a collection of unrelated occurrences. You want the people watching you to care about what occurs next. And doing so entails creating tension. You arouse curiosity, hint at potential outcomes, and maintain the momentum throughout by withholding nothing from the audience. This maintains the attention, intrigue, and hook of your audience.

THE ANSWER YOU PRESENT is the central theme of your story. The solution is a change rather than just an addition to your company. You're altering the rules of the game, not merely fixing an issue. Your story should not feel like a forced sale, but rather like a logical progression of the answer you offer. It must be intuitively clear to the audience that this answer originated from your in-depth comprehension of the issue. It came from living and breathing the problem, from personal insight, and from tenacious pursuit—not from a brainstorming session in a boardroom.

Furthermore, emotion is a key component of storytelling in addition to facts and the tale arc. The tales that evoke strong emotions in people are the ones that they remember. Perhaps it's the success of a tiny company overcoming adversity. Perhaps the invention is what fundamentally altered the way an industry functions. Perhaps it's the picture of a better future—one in which your viewers genuinely experience a sense of inclusion.

Your story should address a topic that goes beyond business, something that is very personal.

Sentimentality isn't the sole thing that makes an emotion. Making individuals feel engaged and a part of something significant is the goal. When written well, your tale speaks to their aspirations, disappointments, and goals. It's not just about your company; it's about how your company operates in their environment.

Identifying Your Unique Selling Proposition (USP)

E very company has that one item that draws customers in, attracts attention, and creates an impression. But once you find it, that's when the magic happens. It goes beyond just a good or service. It is the core, the beating heart of what you have to offer. In the midst of fierce competition, entrepreneurs sometimes lose sight of the one thing that really sets them apart. It's unfortunate because it's generally hiding in plain sight right there.

Your unique selling proposition (USP) may not always be the most conspicuous or vocal aspect of your company. It can be the unmatched level of craftsmanship, the peculiar way you engage with clients, or the unwavering dedication to sustainability that permeates everything you do. Being everything to everyone is not the goal. It's about embracing the one thing that no one else can duplicate, instead.

FINDING THAT ONE THING now is like removing a layer. You begin by taking an outside-in perspective on your company. When someone first encounters you, what do they notice? When they depart, what do they recall? If you're not sure, ask them. It happens that people don't always connect with the thing you consider to be your best quality. Perhaps it's your personal touch in customer service, or perhaps it's your efficient method that makes everything go smoothly. Usually, you've incorporated it into your workflow without appreciating its true worth.

A common mistake made by entrepreneurs is to believe that their offering is unique. And maybe it is, but more often than not, it has to do with the way you provide the good or service. Imagine there are two coffee shops next to each other. Even though they may be selling identical espresso beverages, one is drawing lines around the block. Why? It's the atmosphere, the experience, and the way people feel when they walk in—not the milk or the beans. Their advantage is that.

THAT IS THE DISTINCTION. Similar to this, your USP is what makes people pick you above the competition—not just for the products you sell, but also for the method you market them.

Try to be distinctive rather than better than your competitors in order to find that sweet spot. What defines you as a person? Is it the atmosphere you've established around your company? The manner in which you speak with your clients? Perhaps it's because of the way you've simplified something that was previously difficult for folks to access.

Take out the noise, the buzzwords, and the filler and focus on the important things. It will resonate more strongly the simpler you make it.

Many people make the mistake of trying to sell their company by enumerating every feature and benefit known to man. But nobody has a perfect memory. They remember what sticks. So you want to discover that one thing, that fundamental message that cuts through. It's not about bombarding your audience with information—it's about hitting them with clarity.

It matters to you because this is who we are and what we do. You've hit the mark if you can convey that in a single statement.

Narrative approach is another highly effective method. People enjoy good stories, and stories have the power to bring intangible ideas to life. With a compelling story, your USP will come through. Assume that you launched your company because you felt there was a need for it or because you didn't like the way things were being done. That annoyance?

That's an excellent place to start with your USP. It's what makes your approach different. You're solving an issue that was being ignored, therefore you're more than simply another player in the game. People are significantly more inclined to stick around when they understand why you do what you do.

And keep in mind that your USP doesn't need to be a broad, declarative statement. It might be subdued. Occasionally, the smallest things can have the greatest impact. Maybe you're recognised for lightning-fast customer support.

Perhaps it's the care with which you package every item, giving it the appearance of a gift. Even though they are little, together, they create a distinctive corporate brand that cannot be duplicated.

Everything should go via your USP once you've determined what it is. It serves as the cornerstone of your entire brand and is more than just a sentence on your website or a phrase on your pitch deck. Everything you do, from marketing to customer relations to staff training, should be based on the distinct value you offer.

It's simpler to convey your value when you know exactly what makes you unique. Furthermore, when you effectively convey your value, you begin to gain people's favour even before you ask them for something.

Identifying your USP can occasionally require eliminating unnecessary elements. Entrepreneurs frequently attempt to take on too much, believing that by providing more, they would attract a wider audience. However, this is typically not the case. The more focused you are, the more your audience can grasp what you're about. Focussing more narrowly actually enhances your potential rather than limiting it. It communicates to folks that we are the best at what we do.

Weaving Personal Stories into Your Pitch

Anecdotes from personal experience woven into a pitch have a magnetic quality that draws the listener in like no other. They are honest, genuine, and raw. The reality is, people don't just connect with figures or projections; they connect with the person behind the concept, the road that led to the moment, and the human heartbeat that pushes it forward. A pitch devoid of anecdotal evidence? It lacks the enchantment that solidifies it.

Envision entering a room filled with possible partners or investors. Everyone's there to talk business, but you open with something new, something that rips through the corporate stiffness like a warm blast of wind. Perhaps it was an epiphany you had while trying to address a problem that no one else appeared to care about, or perhaps it was a difficult experience you went through when you first started your business. That tale? It's the hook. It's what transforms your pitch into a dialogue rather than a cold, clinical presentation.

The secret, though, is that personal narratives don't have to be elaborate or extremely dramatic. All they have to do is be real. People are interested in learning how you got here, why this is important to you, and the challenges you faced. Perhaps you were a disgruntled customer, fed up with a dilemma that appeared unsolvable. Or maybe you watched a family business fail as a child and have since discovered a means to create something better.

THESE EXPERIENCES DON'T simply add color—they humanize you and make your mission feel real.

Personal tales are beautiful because they reduce abstract concepts to something concrete. For instance, if you're pitching a tech product, you might be tempted to go into great detail about all the features and benefits of the product. However, that isn't what your audience will remember. What people will recall is the instant you realised how flawed the current system was—perhaps you had to put in a lot of work to complete a straightforward task—and that realisation ignited your desire to develop a better solution. Now, instead of merely talking about the product's technical specs, you're revealing the reason why it exists in the first place.

It's also not only about difficulties. Moments of victory, when you saw you were onto something significant, can be woven into your story. If your company has achieved significant successes, highlighting the personal effects of those achievements can have equal impact.

Did obtaining your first significant client feel like the culmination of all your hard work? Inform them. These successes enable your audience to accompany you on your path, feeling more like participants than mere viewers.

It's also crucial to remember that personal anecdotes enhance the recall value of your pitch. When you leave a presentation with a lot of bullet points, how often have you forgotten what you were supposed to learn? However, stories stick with you. They elicit emotion, and emotion is what drives decision-making. Your tale becomes a thread of narrative that connects your company to something more meaningful than a transaction. There is a link.

The secret to creating a strong pitch is selecting which tale to convey. You must select the personal narrative that best fits the goal of your pitch because not all of them will work for every pitch. When discussing scalability with investors, you may relate a tale about the early stages of your company, when resources were limited but your idea was unstoppable.

However, if you're making a presentation to a group of stakeholders that care about social issues, a narrative about your dedication to moral behaviour may strike a deeper chord.

Additionally, don't be scared to hint at some weakness in your narrative. Authenticity attracts people, and acknowledging your shortcomings and past struggles doesn't make your argument less persuasive—on the contrary, it makes it stronger.

IT DEMONSTRATES THAT you're human, that you've learnt from those events, and that you're stronger because of them. In a pitch, showing vulnerability is an opportunity to establish trust rather than a weakness.

Naturally, the narrative itself shouldn't take front stage in your pitch. Personal anecdotes should support and bolster your primary arguments rather than contradict them. The balance comes from integrating your story directly into the business's objective and vision.

For example, if you're talking about your company's innovative solution, structure the tale around the moment you discovered there was a demand for that solution. This reinforces your point and makes the story more pertinent.

Adding personal anecdotes to your pitch makes you stand out in a crowded field as well. Consider this: while most companies are able to discuss features, benefits, and market potential, not all of them are able to craft a narrative that feels wholly original. Nobody other can tell the same narrative as you.

Its power comes from the fact that it is yours.

Share your story if a personal challenge led to the creation of your business. Let it be apparent whether your vision is firmly based on your upbringing or principles. What sets you apart from other companies that might be providing a comparable service are these stories. Your tale will probably connect with the people you're pitching to more if it is genuine and based on your own experience.

CHAPTER 3
STRUCTURING YOUR PRESENTATION

Imagine yourself in front of a room full of investors, clients, or decision-makers. Their curiosity has created a tension that is fuelled by an electricity in the air, and your only task is to lead them through your world in a way that will inspire them to share your vision and faith in it as much as you do. This is where your pitch's structure turns into an invaluable tool.

A well-planned presentation is designed to take your audience on an entertaining, rational, and emotional journey. It doesn't just happen. And that arrangement? It's the unseen glue that holds everything together and draws in listeners.

First, understand the importance of a compelling opening. You're not just offering them a courteous hello; you're dragging them in with something unexpected. It could be something that makes them sit up and pay attention—a question, a daring comment, or an issue that they can't ignore. Either the first thirty seconds will engage their attention or allow it to wander. Here, it's more about intrigue than it is about confidence. You want to leave them thinking, "Okay, what's coming next?," with an opening that captures their attention.Now is your chance to take command.

What occurs next, though, once you have them in the palm of your hand? Here's where the framework really starts to work. You want to give as clear a definition of the problem as you can following the first hook.

Consider the difficulties that face them, the gaps that must be closed, and the inefficiencies that they have probably seen firsthand but haven't quite put into words. Draw attention to the pain point in a way that resonates with your audience, rather of just framing it as a general problem. You're discussing a real, pressing issue—you're not presenting an idealised picture.

The framework is doing more than simply keeping you organized here—it's moulding their emotional response.

When they feel the problem, they're invested in the solution. And you take them there after that. Move from the problem to the solution with ease. This is not the moment for ambiguity. By talking about the issue and laying out your remedy, you provide a breath of fresh air after creating tension through discussion of the issue. Be convincing, direct, and unambiguous. Not only should you explain your solution to your audience, but also why it is the solution they have been waiting for. Your best ally in this section of the structure is simplicity.

You want them to think, "Yes, this makes sense," and nod in agreement.

However, they won't be engaged by the answer alone forever. Once you've presented it, support it with facts. This is the time to present the information that lends credibility to your pitch—the figures, the outcomes, the hard statistics. While you don't want to bore them with unnecessary details, you do want to be detailed enough for them to understand the significance of what you're saying.

The resources that bolster and authenticate your story are case studies, KPIs, and growth data. Numbers communicate to the logical part of your audience's mind and convey a tale all by themselves. Carefully organise them; don't overwhelm them with information; instead, subtly include figures that support your main arguments.

The "ask," which is arguably the most important component of presentation structure, is next. It's easy to skip over this section, but clarity is key in this situation.

Be explicit when requesting a partnership, investment, or other type of commitment. What are you requiring from them? Why is it necessary for you? What will they receive in exchange? A imprecise or hesitant ask leaves your audience confused. Give them a clear knowledge of what to do next so that they are not left in the dark.

Let's now discuss how you incorporate individuality into this structure. This is how you come across—your tone, your mannerisms, your enthusiasm.

Your individuality adds the muscle, while the structure serves as the framework. Allow your inherent charm, thoughtfulness, or persuasiveness to shine through. Your audience is engaging with you personally; they are not merely listening to a list of things you have to say. In addition, you should maintain a dynamic delivery style even while you adhere to this framework.

Adjust the tempo, change the tone, and make good use of pauses to create suspense or give important points time to register.

Engage with your audience immediately, create eye contact, and talk with passion. Their confidence in you will be strengthened by your assurance in your message.

Consideration should also be given to visual assistance in your structure. They need to enhance rather than overshadow your presentation. The pictures you use should reinforce your message without overshadowing it.

Consider using straightforward, uncomplicated slides that highlight important details or offer a visual summary of intricate data. Keep things simple and never read straight from your slides. Your words should be supported by the images, not the other way around.

Keep the right amount of reasoning and emotion in your pitch. A robust framework makes room for both.

BEGINNINGS AND ENDS frequently place a greater emphasis on emotion in order to engage the audience, inspire them, and arouse their sense of urgency or excitement about your topic. Logic takes the lead in the middle, when you dive into the solution and supporting evidence. However, avoid letting one overpower the other. Weave them together. Maintain the sentimental undertone even when delivering facts. Don't simply let them see the data's impact; let them feel it.

The 60-Second Elevator Pitch

Envision being stranded in a lift with a person who has the power to alter the course of your company. You have less than a minute to leave a lasting impression before the doors close. There's no time for filler or daydreaming—just a succinct, direct message that leaves people captivated and eager for more. That is the basis of the 60-second lift pitch: a condensed, precisely tailored synopsis that, in the time it takes to ride a few floors, gets to the core of your company.

While it may seem easy to write something so brief, it takes skill to convey your point in just one minute. Here, punch and clarity are the objectives. It's imperative that you understand precisely what has to be stated and how to express it loudly enough to be heard. Every phrase counts, and the first thing to focus on is attracting attention quickly. Begin with an attention-grabbing element that sparks interest or elicits a response.

YOUR FIRST LINE OUGHT to ignite the audience, whether it's with a startling statistic, a question that challenges them, or a strong declaration about your market.

After capturing their interest, you can go on to the main focus of your enterprise. Clarity now turns into your greatest ally. Without going into too much detail, you want to make clear to the audience exactly what your company does and why it matters. Many people make the mistake of trying to convey every single detail or nuance in that one minute—cramming too much into it. However, the secret to a strong elevator pitch is to provide just enough details to paint an engaging image rather than stuffing it full of facts.

Consider it as framing an issue along with a possible fix. Your target audience's predicament is the problem, and your company is the answer. In the limited time you have left to paint this painting, simplify it to the bare minimum.

What's the problem, and how are you tackling it in a way that's different or better than everyone else?

This is the point at which your special selling point becomes relevant. Saying what you do is not enough; you also need to explain why it matters. The true hook is that.

But at the same time, avoid making your voice seem forced or artificial. The best lift pitches flow naturally and resemble a dialogue. You are telling a tale, not reading from a script. You want to come across as passionate but not desperate, self-assured but not stiff. The pitch feels genuine, compelling, and human because of that balance.

It flows more the more you practise. However, the goal of that exercise is to master the message so you can deliver it naturally regardless of who you're speaking to or where the conversation is going. It's not about learning lines by heart.

What comes next in the pitch? Make it understandable. It's important that the person you're speaking with knows why they should care. Speaking with a potential investor should focus on how your company will generate revenue and add value rather than merely how it will solve a problem.

When addressing a prospective customer, the focus should be on how your product's features simplify their life rather than its features itself. Always focus on the benefits that the individual in front of you will receive from your pitch.

It's almost time to conclude with a succinct yet impactful message as your 60 seconds are coming to a close. Here's where you provide a brief overview of the benefits your company offers and give them some takeaways.

YOU DON'T WANT TO LEAVE it open-ended or vague; you want to guide them toward the next action, whether it's booking a meeting, getting their card, or simply leaving them wanting to know more. Whatever it is, make sure your closing sentence is just as snappy and memorable as your opener. That way, your pitch will continue to reverberate in their minds long after the lift doors open.

Let us return to a topic that is frequently disregarded: the significance of conciseness.

IT'S TEMPTING TO THINK you need more time to get your point across, yet the power of the elevator pitch lies in its shortness. Making yourself stick to the 60-second time limit helps you focus better. It forces you to cut away the extraneous details and deliver your point more quickly. And when executed properly, that succinctness turns into an asset. Without providing them with too much information, you're just providing enough to keep them interested.

IT'S BENEFICIAL TO divide your pitch into several main sections: a captivating introduction, a concise summary of your company's capabilities, the issue you're trying to solve, the reasons your solution is special, and a compelling conclusion. Each of these elements serves a function, and combined, they build a compact but powerful narrative. Achieving the ideal balance allows your elevator pitch to become a powerful tool in your business toolbox that you can use to impress anyone, anywhere, at any time.

Consider the purpose of your elevator pitch as generating interest rather than trying to sell your complete company. The beauty of it is that it's all about creating a moment where the person on the other side thinks, "I need to know more." You're offering them a preview of what's to come, not a tonne of details.

In those sixty seconds, confidence plays a crucial role as well. Your pitch should sound convincing even if you're still working out some details of your company.

IF THE INDIVIDUAL LISTENING senses any hesitancy, they won't believe in your company. Therefore, speak with conviction when delivering it. Sometimes the words themselves are not as loud as your confidence when it comes to speaking. People tend to remember that. They recall your enthusiasm, your conviction, and your faith in the project you're working on.

Visual Aids and Their Impact

Slides behind you spark to life, but they serve more purposes than aesthetics. They serve as a visual supplement to your speech, drawing the audience's attention to your point of view. And here's the thing: effective use of visual aids can completely change a pitch. Pitch expands beyond just words. It's a firsthand encounter. The ability to translate abstract concepts into something concrete is what gives slides, images, or even a prototype their force.

They provide the audience with a visual element that they can relate to, and this helps to convey ideas more deeply than words could ever hope to.

Finding a balance is the key, though. Too often, presenters overburden their slides with text or bullet points, obscuring the main points with a wall of words. To be honest, nothing makes a room more uninterested than someone reading aloud from a slide, word for word. The eyes drift away, the mind checks out. It would be as if you were speaking to yourself.

Visual aids should augment, not replace, your words; rather, they should work as a co-pilot to help you convey your point. This implies that much like your pitch, your slides must be precise and targeted. The game-changers are a few powerful pictures, a graph that emphasises a crucial idea, or a prototype that everyone can't stop staring at.

When utilised properly, slides have a certain weight. Consider the elegance of a picture that conveys a message more quickly than any words could .

A graph that all of a sudden clarifies a difficult idea. A prototype that's been waiting for everyone in the room to get their hands on. Visuals contribute this mixture of engagement and expectation. But when developing those slides, it's crucial to remember: less is more. There's no need to overload the viewers with ten information-dense slides. Rather, visualise every slide as a potent blow. Just one picture. Just one message. One thing to remember.

BETTER YET, CONSIDER your visual aids or slides as an additional rhythm to your pitch's flow. Maybe when you discuss the issue, a graphic, unsettling picture evokes that particular point of suffering. Upon selecting the solution, the screen abruptly illuminates with a clear, uncomplicated image illustrating how your product addresses the issue. An image that strengthens the message is used to break up each section. Not to outdo it, not to outcompete it. merely deepening the already stated points.

These days, the effectiveness of visual aids frequently depends on how they are delivered. One could be tempted to believe that flashier is better. Who doesn't adore an amazing demo or a sleek animation, after all? But relevancy is everything. Even though a nicely designed presentation could draw attention, it is meaningless if it doesn't further the story you are trying to tell. Prototypes, too? When used properly, they are pure gold. People find that a product seems more real when they see it in person.

All of a sudden, the topic you are discussing is in front of them and not just a concept. But, if you're going to whip out a prototype, it needs to be the proper moment. The last thing you want is for your words to become lost in the spotlight as the audience concentrates on a spectacular demo.

When visual aids only accomplish one thing, it is to stimulate the senses. The objective is always to capture attention, whether it is through the slick layout of a slide, the sensitive feel of a prototype, or simply a quick film that breaks up the monotony of speaking. That being said, not every pitch has to be a high-key affair. Simplicity is essential sometimes. Simple graphics like a well-crafted graph or image can have just as much impact as elaborate product demonstrations.

Understanding your audience is key. For example, statistics, projections, and financials presented in clear, readable graphs or charts may be warmly received by investors.

However, showcasing how your product feels, looks, or works in the actual world may be more beneficial for a pitch that is centred on the needs of the customer. Never forget that the person seated across from you is there to service the pitch, not the other way around, so adjust your visual aids accordingly.

Though they can capture attention, images shouldn't be used as a crutch. You can have the most amazing pictures in the world, but if your message isn't clear, they won't save you. The purpose of visual aids is to elucidate, support, and bolster.

However, you always steal the show from them. They are the flavouring, not the meal. It's your words, your presence, and your passion that really make the concept stick. Visuals simply assist in completing the task. They offer you a small advantage and a means of making your proposal visible rather than just heard.

Let's now discuss keeping the audience's interest. A visually stimulating tool that modifies at the ideal time and elegantly presents a new idea keeps the audience interested.

Audiences are naturally drawn to what's on screen, and engagement increases when the content on the screen corresponds with what you're saying.

All of a sudden, you're leading your audience through an experience rather than merely making a presentation. They are taking in information as well as listening.

However, there's a mistake to be aware of here: relying too much on slides. The moment you start leaning on them too strongly, you lose the room. Individuals begin to focus on the screen instead of you when they stop looking at you, and before you know it, they're zoning out and reading ahead. That poses a risk. It is what you want—people interested in you, not a bunch of words on a PowerPoint. Maintain simple, concise, and impactful slides. Instead of taking over your narrative, they are there to highlight it.

It's also critical to keep in mind that visual aids can produce moments that are unforgettable. Consider this: knowledge is better retained by individuals when it is heard as well as seen.

So when you throw up a presentation with a great image or bring out a prototype, you're reinforcing your message in a way that stays. All of a sudden, it's not just something they heard; it's something they saw and felt.

CHAPTER 4
ENGAGING YOUR AUDIENCE

Imagine that as soon as you enter a room, everyone's eyes flit to you. This is the critical instant when interaction occurs and the spark that ignites or extinguishes the connection between you and your audience. It's not about giving lectures or reciting facts like a machine. Without the audience realising it, it's a show and a discourse.

HOW THEN CAN YOU ENTICE them in? The first step is to scan the space, determine the atmosphere, and make quick adjustments. This is not a script of magic. Your enthusiasm establishes the mood, and the way you make the pitch will either draw them in or cause them to lose interest. A monotone delivery kills the buzz, no matter how excellent the product or service is. Your voice has a certain power about it; the pauses, rises, and falls draw listeners in like a magnet. People pay attention when your passion shines through, even in tiny amounts.

Their eyes latch onto you because you've just made it personal, not some one-way broadcast they're forced to sit through.

It's not just a matter of speaking *at* them anymore. Even if they aren't speaking, the finest pitches elicit a sense of participation from the audience. Here, maintaining eye contact is crucial. Glance around the room, make eye contact with several people. Give them the impression that you are talking directly to them and that your pitch was created with them in mind. And watch for the body language.

Taking a step back? Embraced with crossed arms? It's time to change strategies. Even if it's only in their minds, ask a question that will startle them into joining in by leaning in and getting closer. Engagement is an invisible thread, and every word or gesture is a tug to keep them attached to you.

Narrative serves as a conduit for interaction. Explaining a product's characteristics and listing its advantages is one thing, but what if your pitch also includes a sympathetic story? You're cooking now. People remember stories.

They identify with the story and experience the associated feelings; all of a sudden, your product is more than simply a fix; it becomes a part of their reality. Creating a narrative brings your words to life, whether it's a brief personal narrative or a customer success story. It becomes something tangible, something they can grasp, and ceases to be an abstract concept.

These small sparks can turn a flat tone into a dynamic experience. Give them a thought-provoking question to start with, even if they choose not to respond out loud. Plant it like a seed.

Without them even realising it, it involves them. It changes the dynamic if it is timed correctly. Instead of passively taking it all in, the audience is actively involved, leaning in, and anticipating what will happen next. And since we're on the subject of questions, let's flip it. You must also be prepared for theirs. When the hands go up or the eyebrows rise with a question that's just waiting to be asked, you've reached a sweet spot. After all, engagement is a two-way street.

THE GRAPHICS CAN HELP here, too. A thoughtfully positioned slide that emphasises your idea without drawing attention to itself. Perhaps it's a graph that makes the data hard to ignore or an image that strikes at the heart of emotions. These aren't simply for décor; they're a technique to yank attention back whenever it starts to slip. Nobody wants to sit through a slide deck that looks like a wall of text, so keep them brief, to the point, and punchy. Your comments should be supported by the images, not contradicted by them. It all comes down to that balance.

Now let's discuss the dynamics of the room. You must take ownership of the area without taking over. The true beauty of a presentation occurs when the listener feels engaged, but far too many pitches sound like a monologue. Walk the room if it feels natural, alter your position, keep the vibe alive. It's all in the way you move, make eye contact, and subtly convey to everyone that they're part of something spectacular. Make the most of the space. Sometimes all it takes to draw an audience into your orbit is to take a step closer to them.

It transforms a passive presentation into an active dialogue by tearing down the perceived barrier separating the speaker and the audience.

The power of silence is another. When used appropriately, pauses can speak more than words. It allows the message to sink in and provides the audience a chance to catch up and process what you've spoken. All too frequently, presenters hurriedly pack material into every second of their speeches as if they were scared of silence. But deepening interaction happens in silence.

The crowd leans in, anticipating what will happen next when you pause. It builds tension and provides a little pause for the moment to fully register.

Although not everyone has the humour to lighten the mood, a well-placed joke can work wonders. It eases the tension, humanises the pitch, and increases your relatability. It's not necessary to laugh at yourself all the time, but occasionally a little self-awareness, a joke that makes light of the situation, or a statement that acknowledges the audience can help you and the audience get along better. They are with you, not just observing. Though it's a slight change, it makes viewers become participants.

Not to be overlooked is excitement. Your conviction in the idea you're pitching must be genuine; it cannot be faked. Between passion and over-excitation, there is a thin line. If you overdo it, it will sound like a pitch. If it's too little, it will appear as though you don't even trust your own creation. When it's sincere, enthusiasm spreads easily, and people can tell when something is real.

It's in the way you talk about the idea, the product, the service—it has to feel like you live and breathe it. The passion in the room has a contagious impact.

Engagement is about connection. It matters more how you make them feel than what you say. The goal is for the audience to leave the room feeling moved, not knowing every single detail about your pitch. Motivated. Curious. thrilled. Figures and facts can be added later.

IT MATTERS THAT PEOPLE are paying attention to you and that they are walking away from your speech with your words still ringing in their ears.

The goal is to pique the audience's curiosity without overloading them with details. You don't have to respond to every query that may come up throughout the pitch. That isn't the purpose of this moment. Your goal is to pique their interest, arouse their curiosity, and provide just enough information to entice them to carry on the conversation.

Reading the Room-
Body Language and Presence

When you enter into a room to pitch your business, the energy humming in the air isn't just about the words streaming from your mouth. It's all about the nonverbal cues: your commanding presence, your eye contact, and your body language. These components combine to create a complex web of nonverbal cues that have the power to quickly strengthen or weaken your pitch.

IT'S SIMILAR TO THE hidden ingredient that amplifies the flavour of your message, giving it more resonance and pop.

Consider this: even before you speak, the way you carry yourself can convey a message. Arms crossed or slouching conveys a protective or insecure message. Alternatively, visualise assuming a tall, confident stance with your shoulders back. The way you stand tells your audience that you are not merely providing information; rather, you genuinely believe what you are saying.

People are drawn to you and are drawn into your orbit by that inexplicable charm.

And there's the power of making eye contact. When you look someone in the eye, a bridge or instant connection is formed. It demonstrates your presence, engagement, and sincere interest in the discussion. Maintaining eye contact communicates openness, honesty, and trust. However, too much can have a strong, even frightening sense.

A SENSATION OF INCLUSION is created by finding that sweet spot—quickly scanning the room and making eye contact with several individuals. Instead than feeling like bystanders, everyone feels like they are a part of the story.

Body language goes beyond just posture and eye contact. It's all in the little motions and facial expressions you use to accentuate your words. Your delivery gains vitality when you accent a point with your hands. Leaning in or giving a simple nod might convey agreement and promote conversation.

Your body is the rhythm and your words the melody, combining to give your audience a perfect experience. On the other hand, fidgeting or staying still can make your message less effective. It conveys a sense of unease or trepidation. You should move with purpose, be engaged, and be flowing. Every movement you make should add to your story, not take away from it.

The presence you bring into the room is another crucial component. It's that vibe you give off, a blend of warmth, approachability, and confidence.

Are you a happy person when you walk in? Do you come across as friendly and open, or as closed off? A friendly grin may disarm even the toughest crowd. It creates a welcoming atmosphere, making individuals more receptive to your views. However, it must be sincere. A fake smile is insufficient. Genuineness is a magnetic quality that draws others in and makes them feel at ease.

Speaking is not as vital as listening. There's more to reading the room than merely putting on your best pitch.

It all comes down to observing the responses of your audience. Do they have a leaned-in, nodding, or distracted expression at their phones? Changing your strategy in response to these signs can have a profound impact. If you perceive disinterest, it could be time to turn. Make sure the question you ask draws them back into the discussion. Change it from a monologue to a conversation to promote involvement and interaction.

ANOTHER FACET OF YOUR presence is the variation of your voice. Your voice's tone, pitch, and tempo can all have a big impact on how your message is understood. You'll lose an audience with a monotone speech faster than you can blink. However, you can produce a resonant emotional cadence by modulating your voice, which involves speaking softly at important points and then accelerating the speed for emphasis. Your voice carries captivating passion that entices listeners to join in on your excitement.

Moreover, mirroring body language can strengthen bonds. A sense of unity is created by subtly mirroring the posture and gestures of your audience. If they're leaning in, you can lean in, too. If they seem at ease, go with the flow. You all recognise that this is a shared understanding and have come to a quiet agreement. But be cautious. Excessive use of it may come across as false. Not imitation, but rapport-building is the aim.

KEEP IN MIND THAT GESTURES and body language can convey cultural subtleties. Something that is effective in one context could not be in another. Being aware of these distinctions demonstrates attentiveness and respect and enables you to modify your pitch as necessary. It exhibits a professionalism that says a lot about your personality. It's about demonstrating that you're not only a speaker who can fit any audience. Your audience will feel heard and noticed if you are able to read the room and make adjustments.

When it's time to conclude your pitch, think about what you want to say one last time. It really important how your presentation ends. Making a strong impression can be achieved by standing erect, maintaining eye contact with your audience, and concluding with assurance. It serves to emphasise your points and serves as a reminder to everyone of what you said. A compelling conclusion brings the story to a satisfying close and keeps the audience interested rather than eager to go on.

Handling Questions and Objections

During a pitch, navigating the terrain of enquiries and detractors can resemble tightrope walking. Using a combination of calmness, confidence, and planning is necessary to convert possible obstacles into chances for more in-depth interaction. When you get ready for this portion of your presentation, you're not just practicing your responses; you're strengthening your case and proving that you can withstand criticism.

THE MOOD IS SET WITH anticipation. Put yourself in the audience's position. What worries might they have? What gaps in comprehension could arise? By placing yourself in their shoes, you can be ready for any queries they could have. It's a bit like playing chess; you need to anticipate several moves ahead, foreseeing the arguments before they even appear.

Practicing your answers once you've identified potential questions will help you feel more confident.

Practicing out loud, possibly in front of a friend or coworker, helps to clarify unclear concepts into well-organised arguments. This practice helps you seem more natural and fluid in your responses while also improving your linguistic skills. Instead of reading from a script, you want to seem as though the responses come from your area of expertise.

Tone matters immensely. Your response to enquiries has the power to start a conversation or end one. Keeping your composure and manner open facilitates a cordial conversation.

Consider concerns as insightful input rather than as personal assaults. Listen carefully when someone expresses a concern. Keep your eyes open, nod in agreement, and convey sincere interest. This confirms their viewpoint and shows them to be respected. Saying something like, "That's a great question," in response, establishes a collaborative tone and fosters rapport.

Reiterating your stance and giving your audience a sense of being heard are the goals of responding to concerns, not winning a debate.

Before responding, acknowledge their worry. For example, if someone doubts your business model's viability, start by understanding their doubts. "I understand why you might feel that way, given the current market conditions," you could reply. Then, provide proof or instances to refute their worries. To support your arguments, provide statistics, testimonies, or case studies. This combination of recognition and proof turns the conversation from combative to productive.

IN SOME CIRCUMSTANCES, you may not have a quick answer. That is entirely appropriate. You may reply, "That's a valid point, and I want to make sure I give you the most accurate information," as opposed to stumbling through an unsure response. This technique not only preserves your credibility but also shows that you appreciate their perspective enough to look for a considered response. Let's follow up on it following our talk. It demonstrates a dedication to excellence and honesty.

IT CAN ALSO BE QUITE beneficial to turn objections into conversations. Whenever someone questions your pricing, ask them to discuss value with you rather than responding with a defensive explanation of your cost structure. Pose open-ended enquiries such as, "What price scheme do you think is better appropriate for our services?"Talking to them face-to-face encourages cooperation and can even spark unexpected insights in the conversation."

BY PROMOTING A TWO-way dialogue, it positions you as a collaborator rather than merely a seller.

Reframing the objection can also be a powerful tactic. If someone in the audience questions your anticipated progress, turn their doubt into a chance.

"While I acknowledge that growth can seem ambitious, it's driven by trends we're seeing in our industry," one could reply. This changes the argument into a starting point for talking about the advantages of your business model and competitive position in the market.

"Let's explore how those trends are shaping our strategies."

It's also important to develop a "bank" of powerful responses for repeating themes in objections. Whether it's about budgetary restraints, market saturation, or competition, feeling prepared to address any problem that comes up is enhanced by having a bank of thoughtful responses. Consider these as tools in your toolbox; the more adaptable the items in your collection, the more equipped you are to handle a range of situations.

Remember that your body language during this phase has a huge influence.

Keep your arms extended and do not adopt a defensive position. Leaning slightly forward conveys curiosity and involvement. Together with your spoken words, these nonverbal clues support your message that you're here to assist, not to argue.

It's critical to keep an eye on the room's atmosphere as the conversation progresses. Shifting the topic of discussion might help reduce tension if you notice it.

If used sparingly, humour can occasionally be a nice way to lighten the mood.

THE IDEA IS TO ESTABLISH a laid-back atmosphere where everyone feels at ease discussing their ideas.

Once every query has been answered, it can be helpful to summarise the main ideas. This serves to both support and gently redirect the discussion back to the advantages of your pitch. To reinforce your earlier remarks and provide your audience a clear takeaway, you may say something like, "So, to recap, we've identified some challenges, but our innovative solutions uniquely position us to tackle these effectively."

CHAPTER 5
THE FOLLOW-UP STRATEGY

Developing a follow-up plan turns a strong pitch into an impactful one. You don't want to put so much effort into the presentation and then have it end in quiet. The follow-up builds relationships that have the potential to develop into successful partnerships by acting as a link between the initial excitement and further discussions.

IN THIS CASE, TIMING is crucial. Reaching contact as soon as possible after the pitch demonstrates zeal and dedication. A timely follow-up maintains the momentum, whereas waiting too long runs the danger of letting the spark fade. Imagine that 24 or 48 hours following the meeting, you send a message. This period of time helps your main points to stay in line with their ideas and keeps you at the forefront of their minds. It's all about striking while the iron is hot and stoking the enthusiasm that the presentation created.

You should prioritise personalisation in your follow-up correspondence. A generic email is insufficient. Rather, focus on the particular exchanges that occurred during the pitch. Maybe someone brought up a specific difficulty they have in their line of work. Make mention of that in your message: "I valued your observations regarding [particular issue]. This level of attention to detail establishes rapport and reassures them that you are a sincere partner interested in their particular circumstance, not simply another pitch.

I think our solution can really address that.

Thank them without coming across as too formal. A brief but sincere "thank you" makes a big difference. It shows that you value their time and consideration and goes beyond simple courtesy. In your follow-up, acknowledge their contributions to the conversation. Making a specific reference to something they said establishes a rapport and supports the notion that you were genuinely interested. Saying something like, "I found your perspective on [topic] really enlightening," can start a deeper discussion.

Your follow-up becomes an opportunity rather than just a formality if you provide value. Provide other materials, perspectives, or pertinent articles that complement the conversation. You may submit a current research or report that adds more perspective if you talked about industry trends. By using this strategy, you establish yourself as a thought leader and someone who goes above and beyond.

IT'S ABOUT SHOWING them that you care about their achievement by adding value without being overbearing.

The follow-up channel you select can change based on how you communicated at first. The most popular method is still email, which provides a formal but friendly means of communication. But if your connection permits, think about using more informal networks like LinkedIn or even just giving someone a call. Every medium has an own tone, so choosing the appropriate one shows how well you understand the nature of the relationship.

Clarity is key while writing the message. Instead of writing long paragraphs, try to make succinct but powerful assertions. Information can be better organised with the use of bulleted lists, which will assist the reader quickly understand your important points. A planned follow-up keeps things from getting overwhelmed while still giving them all the information they need. Recall that being clear indicates professionalism and consideration for their time.

OUTLINING THE NEXT steps can be very successful in gaining the interest of individuals who exhibited interest throughout the pitch. Be proactive in moving the subject along, whether it's by setting up a demonstration, another meeting, or more information. The way you phrase things counts; rather than just saying what you want to happen, frame it as a chance for cooperation.

"Are you available for a second meeting next week to discuss this in more detail?"invites conversation and places a focus on collaboration.

Addressing concerns raised by the pitch? Don't be afraid to bring them up in your follow-up. Mention any topics you didn't cover in detail and provide further information. This approach shows a dedication to openness and a readiness to take on obstacles head-on. It demonstrates your appreciation for their worries and your readiness to have a meaningful conversation.

It is imperative that you maintain organisation in your follow-up plan. Consider using a CRM application or a basic spreadsheet to track your efforts.

Future interactions can be facilitated by keeping a record of the questions asked, the pledges made, and the topics of interest expressed by each stakeholder during the pitch. With this well-planned strategy, you can effectively customise your follow-ups and steer clear of generic messages that could turn off recipients.

Including a call to action is still necessary. Make sure the message is appealing rather than aggressive as you direct the receiver towards the next steps.

USE PHRASES LIKE "WHAT'S the best time for you to connect again?" or "I look forward to hearing your thoughts.""invites additional conversation without being intrusive. It highlights how important their opinions are and maintains the flow of the discourse.

Including several touchpoints in the digital age can help strengthen your follow-up plan. Consider establishing a social media connection or participating in their postings after sending them an email. This method produces a multi-layered exchange that encourages comfort.

Every touchpoint deepens the bond between you and the other person by gently reminding them of you.

Following up on the original pitch, it's critical to monitor the direction of the conversation. Do not be afraid to send a polite reminder if, following your follow-up, you receive no response. Just a short note saying, "I wanted to follow up on my earlier message. Reengaging them without seeming frantic, "I'm excited to continue our discussion," It all comes down to identifying the ideal balance between professionalism and perseverance.

Maintaining open lines of communication is still essential later on. These exchanges keep the relationship friendly, whether it's via exchanging success stories, providing sporadic updates about your company, or just checking in. Instead of chasing a deal nonstop, the goal should be to cultivate a relationship that will grow when the right circumstances come together.

Creating a Post-Pitch Action Plan

After a pitch, following up turns an exhilarating moment into a long-lasting partnership. For entrepreneurs, a post-pitch action plan serves as a road map, preventing the initial excitement from fading into silence. During this stage, you should strengthen ties and maintain dialogue to encourage stakeholders to interact with your vision.

First, in this game, timing is everything. Send a thank-you note within 24 to 48 hours of finishing your pitch.

This prompt reply expresses your gratitude for their time while capturing the essence of the moment. A heartfelt thank-you creates a positive impression, reminding stakeholders that their attention is valued. Even though it can be as small as a quick email, this action has a big impact on building rapport.

Although gratitude creates the foundation, the momentum is maintained by the subsequent content. Think back to what you discovered during the pitch.

Has anyone shown interest in learning more about a particular facet of your company? This is your opportunity to excel. In your follow-up correspondence, make reference to those points and make a connection to your earlier conversation. It's like picking up where you left off, signaling that you are genuinely engaged and attentive.

It changes the game to add value now. This is the time to share any case studies or articles that you mentioned during the pitch.

INCLUDE PERTINENT LINKS in your content that will help your audience learn more. Whether it's a long report or a quick read, adding more details strengthens your reputation as an informed partner. By being proactive and demonstrating your interest in their comprehension of your company, you build rapport with them while also enhancing your credibility.

Here, personalisation is really important. Every follow-up ought to feel customized—almost as though it was made just for that individual.

Making a special mention during your conversation increases its impact. "I liked our discussion on [particular subject]. A generic note doesn't have the same resonance as "I thought you might find this article interesting." It elevates an ordinary message to a meaningful exchange that strengthens the bond between the two parties.

When writing your thank-you note, try to be as concise and clear as possible. Stay courteous but professional at the same time. Don't overpower them with long paragraphs.

Instead, concentrate on using succinct sentences to clearly convey your ideas. You can demonstrate that you are a methodical and considerate communicator by sending them a well-structured message that is both easy to read and respectful of their time.

After the initial thank-you, the next step involves outlining any additional information you promised during the pitch. Clearly state what you want to offer, whether it's a financial forecast, a market analysis, or a product demonstration.

"I'll follow up with the detailed market analysis we discussed, and I'm happy to set up a time for a product demonstration," demonstrates your commitment to transparency and thoroughness.

Creating a post-pitch action plan requires a clear set of next steps. This plan serves as a guide for both you and the recipient, helping to maintain momentum. A collaborative mentality works wonders here. Instead of just declaring your intentions, allow the recipient to participate in the process.

"Would it be possible to schedule a follow-up call next week to discuss your thoughts on the market analysis?" encourages engagement and shows you value their input.

Organizing your action plan is crucial. Consider using a checklist or timetable to keep track of commitments made during the pitch. This arrangement helps you remember what information has to be conveyed, as well as when to contact out again. It prevents the "oops, I forgot" moment, helping you to remain on top of things while exhibiting your professionalism.

Addressing any potential concerns from the pitch can also fit into your follow-up approach. If objections were voiced, acknowledge them in your correspondence. "I understand your concerns about [specific issue]. I want to provide more understanding around that." This approach shows that you're not just brushing aside objections; you're ready to tackle them head-on. This transparency creates trust and deepens the partnership.

AS YOU ESTABLISH THIS post-pitch conversation, remember to measure the recipient's engagement. Pay attention to their responses and tone. Are they enthusiastic? Reserved? Adjust your strategy accordingly. If they exhibit interest in diving deeper, be prepared to share extra insights. On the flip side, if their responses are brief, try taking a more soft approach in future conversations.

Implementing a follow-up schedule helps preserve the relationship over time. Plan periodic check-ins that extend beyond the immediate aftermath of the pitch. Whether it's giving industry news, corporate updates, or inviting them to events, keeping the lines of communication open creates continued involvement. These connections communicate that you're not simply interested in a one-off pitch but in developing a lifelong engagement.

In the digital age, employing technology can strengthen your follow-up plan. Consider using CRM tools to track conversations and set reminders for follow-ups. This level of organization prevents potential oversight and helps ensure that no topic falls between the cracks. Additionally, using email tracking software can give insights into when your messages are opened, allowing you to time your follow-ups more successfully.

As time passes, the purpose remains clear: keep fostering the relationship. If you detect curiosity but don't receive immediate responses, don't hesitate to follow up again. A simple message noting, "Just wanted to touch base to see if you had a chance to review the information I sent," can keep the conversation alive without sounding intrusive.

Building Long-Term Relationships with Stakeholders

Nurturing ties with stakeholders beyond mere commerce. It's about constructing a fabric of trust, collaboration, and shared vision. This dance of involvement transforms casual encounters into lifelong connections. When you engage time and effort into these friendships, the rewards often appear in unexpected yet profound ways.

CONSISTENT COMMUNICATION becomes the lifeblood of these relationships. Picture a garden; if you water it consistently, the plants thrive. Here, the same idea holds true. Inform your stakeholders of your accomplishments, difficulties, and development. Emails, newsletters, and even informal coffee dates can serve as regular updates. The objective? Maintain visibility and relevancy in their minds.

Although they can be a useful tool, emails don't have to be a hassle. Give them individuality and sincerity.

Provide updates on your business as well as personal reflections on your travels. The statement, "We faced a setback last month, but it taught us valuable lessons," humanises the situation and elicits an emotional response from the audience. They wish to feel like more than simply a name on a list—that they are a part of your journey.

Adjust your message to the intended audience. Acknowledge that the interests and priorities of various stakeholders differ. While a partner might be more interested in operational efficiency, an investor might be more concerned with financial growth. Creating customised messages can greatly increase your outreach's efficacy. Instead of sending out a general update, focus on the points that each person finds most meaningful. This approach exhibits respect for their time and a deep grasp of their reasons.

A consistent communication rhythm contributes to the vitality of partnerships. Striking a balance is crucial, though; while regular updates are helpful, avoid providing too much information.

Decide on a timetable that is convenient for all parties involved. While making sure you're not overstuffing their inboxes, you can build anticipation with monthly newsletters or quarterly check-ins.

Never undervalue the influence of casual conversations. These are frequently the most insightful times. Informal conversations over coffee or a brief phone contact can disclose a lot about the expectations and values of stakeholders.

THROUGH THESE EXCHANGES, a feeling of community is cultivated and the notion that you are all travelling together is strengthened. Throughout these conversations, show real curiosity. Pose open-ended enquiries and pay close attention. This technique fosters a friendly relationship and an honest conversation.

Addressing obstacles is just as crucial as celebrating accomplishments. Communication that is genuine builds trust. Inform your stakeholders when something goes wrong.

They value openness, particularly when they can tell you're trying to find a solution. Talking about the challenges you're facing demonstrates your dedication to development and fortitude. This frank attitude not only develops connections but also inspires stakeholders to assist you through bad times.

Think about how important it is to include stakeholders in your decision-making procedures. Ask for their opinions on upcoming projects or possible difficulties. They are more inclined to become emotionally invested in your achievement when they perceive that their opinions count. How do you feel about our new approach to launching a product?"invites cooperation and conveys your appreciation for their knowledge. Having a sense of ownership over your path might make you go from being passive viewers to active participants.

Your outreach efforts can be amplified by social media. A wider audience can be reached by posting updates, insights, and success stories on social media sites like LinkedIn.

REGULAR POSTING KEEPS you visible and serves as a reminder to stakeholders of your involvement and progress. Additionally, it encourages engagement; likes, comments, and shares open doors to expand relationships through meaningful conversations.

Never undervalue the significance of personal touches. Small gestures or handwritten letters can make a big impression. After a meeting, a straightforward thank-you card can express gratitude in a way that digital communication frequently cannot.

These actions show that you genuinely care about the partnership, making it an unforgettable experience that both parties will treasure.

Industry conferences and networking events are excellent venues for building relationships. Attend events where you can expect the presence of your stakeholders. Take use of this time to catch up, give updates, and brainstorm new concepts. Virtual meetings may lack the spirit of camaraderie that in-person interactions provide.

THESE INTERACTIONS might result in unforeseen partnerships and insights, so approach them with excitement and curiosity.

Feedback turns into a potent ally in the development of relationships. Establish an environment of open communication where interested parties are at ease discussing your progress. Request feedback on your project or proposal so that you can make improvements. This proactive strategy shows your dedication to development and adaptability.

Stakeholders get more deeply invested in your journey when they perceive that their opinions have an impact on your decisions.

Furthermore, celebrate accomplishments together. Recognise accomplishments with your stakeholders, no matter how minor. A straightforward "We've hit our sales goal!" shared in an email or a celebratory lunch can create a sense of shared accomplishment. These happy times strengthen ties and build a positive story around your relationship.

MAKE USE OF DATA TO enlighten stakeholders. Sharing important indicators that demonstrate success or development can pique curiosity and create excitement. Instead of just declaring that your firm is doing well, give captivating images or statistics that convey a story. Progress can be effectively communicated via graphs, charts, or infographics, which also make the content easier to read and comprehend.

CHAPTER 6
LEARNING FROM EXPERIENCE

Every experience, no matter how good or bad, has lessons to be learnt. Your entire company plan and your approach to pitching are shaped by the lessons you take away from these experiences. Taking stock of previous experiences might help you make innovative discoveries and improve your approach.

FREQUENTLY, THE TRIP begins with a poorly executed pitch. Imagine speaking spontaneously while in front of possible investors, but the exchange feels forced. Interrogations surface, brows wrinkle, and the enthusiasm you had planned fades. This situation may hurt, yet it presents opportunities for development. Analyse the encounter. What caused the disconnect? Was it the message's clarity? The degree of interaction with your images? Maybe it was the vibe of the audience that you misinterpreted. These questions help you advance.

Try making a note of your observations right away following each pitch. What struck a chord? What gave way? This instantaneous reflection helps to capture unfiltered ideas before they get lost in the bustle of day-to-day work life. Create a specific journal for pitches, capturing everything from the questions asked to the non-verbal indications you witnessed. Patterns start to show up over time, helping you to improve your strategy.

REVIEW THE INPUT PROVIDED by team members and stakeholders. During your lecture, did they show signs of confusion? Or perhaps they thought some parts were really interesting? Accept criticism as a treasure. It presents a novel viewpoint, highlighting blind spots that may escape your notice. Foster an environment of open communication, which is crucial for development, by allowing honest and constructive criticism.

AFTER EVERY PITCH, think about setting up feedback sessions with your team. Talk about what went well, what didn't, and how we can do better in the future. Establish a friendly environment where everyone feels at ease discussing ideas throughout these sessions. By working together, you not only improve your pitches going forward but also develop team dynamics because everyone is motivated by the group's success as a whole.

UNEXPECTED INSIGHTS can arise from thinking back on past experiences. Lessons can often be learnt most richly from what appears to be a setback. A squandered chance may encourage you to explore different techniques, pushing you outside your comfort zone. For instance, you can delve further into your market research following a poor pitch in order to find insights that motivate a fresh approach. Resilience is a feature that investors and stakeholders admire, and this adaptability proves it.

KEEP A JOURNAL OF YOUR travels and the lessons you've learnt. Make a graphic map that shows the key points in your growth trajectory. This might serve as a motivational reminder during hard times. When you're feeling self-conscious, looking back at these achievements shows you how far you've come and the abilities you've acquired. No matter how tiny, acknowledge and celebrate these wins because they add to the story that is developing about you.

ACCEPT THE IDEA THAT your pitching approach needs to be iterated. Every presentation serves as a template for the one after it, letting you experiment with alternative strategies, polish your story, and increase audience participation. What worked for one audience might not work for another, creating a never-ending cycle of progress. Experiment with varied storytelling strategies, modifying your tone, and even including multimedia aspects. Consider each pitch as a chance to improve.

THE VALUE OF PREPARATION becomes abundantly clear as you gain experience. Examining winning pitches can provide you an idea of what made them work. Analyzing the strategies utilised, the structure followed, and the engagement levels obtained offers a blueprint for future presentations. Were there any interesting anecdotes in the winning pitches? Were there any powerful images? Make a note of these elements and add them to your own structure.

MAKING CONNECTIONS with colleagues in your field might also yield insightful viewpoints. Attend industry gatherings, conferences, or workshops and have discussions about pitching techniques. Hearing about the experiences, triumphs, and setbacks of others produces a wealth of information that can be utilised. This group serves as a sounding board for ideas, enabling you to modify and try out newly discovered insights.

LEARNING PROGRESSES when a curious mindset is fostered. Consider every experience as a chance to improve. When faced with obstacles, consider what you can learn from them rather than focussing on the negative.With this mental adjustment, you can accept even the most difficult situations as opportunities for growth.

Including role-playing in your preparation process might have a lot of unexpected advantages. Colleagues should participate in simulated pitches where they can play investors or stakeholders.

Encourage them to ask hard questions or voice objections. This exercise builds your confidence and gets you ready for situations that may arise in the real world. When you practise managing challenging situations, the unpredictable nature of live pitching becomes less daunting.

As you build your pitching talents, pay attention to the progression of your narrative. Which tales speak to you? What moments spark passion? Using real-life stories in your presentations helps you establish a closer emotional bond with your audience. Your vision becomes more clear and engaging as a result of your sincerity.

In your pitch, honour the craft of storytelling. Share your journey, the struggles you've experienced, and the victories you've gained. This story gives stakeholders a glimpse into your passion and highlights the human aspect of your company. They become invested in your path when they can relate to your experience, which frequently results in stronger relationships.

Analyzing Pitch Outcomes

Reflecting on pitch outcomes serves as a great tool for growth and development. Whether or not a meeting with potential stakeholders is successful, there are always insights to be discovered. By compiling these experiences, improvement strategies become more tangible from abstract teachings.

Let's start by visualising the rush of adrenaline that precedes a pitch. There's that moment of expectancy, the audience's gaze locked in, and the stakes feel huge.

The initial excitement might quickly give way to a flurry of feelings when everything has settled, particularly if the desired result wasn't achieved. Accept that whirlwind of emotions; there is a lot of knowledge to be found there. Whether you are met with cheers or quiet, it's time to stand back and evaluate the situation.

Start by writing down your initial thoughts following the pitch. Which sections felt flawless? What circumstances made you hesitate? Seize those ephemeral moments before they disappear.

We will build on this post-pitch thought in order to do a more thorough analysis in the future. A simple journal dedicated to this purpose can be essential, allowing you to document your trip and identify growth over time.

Think about asking your team or reliable colleagues for their opinions. Their viewpoints can highlight details you would have missed. Have open dialogue with them regarding the pitch. What were they able to witness? Which segments seemed to resonate?

Remember that this process depends on openness, so ask them for their honest thoughts. These discussions might highlight recurrent themes and patterns that you may have missed.

As you present, keep a close eye on how the audience is responding. Facial expressions, body language, and degree of participation all convey a lot. Did they get really excited about a certain part, or did they fidget when you brought up a new concept? These indicators offer a road map for navigating your upcoming pitches.

Understanding how to read your audience boosts your capacity to personalise your message, producing a more fascinating experience.

You may improve your talents even more by dissecting particular components of your pitch. Think about the ways you tell stories. Were your tales believable and captivating? Did you adequately describe the issue that your company seeks to resolve? This analysis takes delivery style into account in addition to content. Reflect on your tone, pacing, and energy.

Exuberance can create a sense of excitement, yet composure can foster trust. Strike a balance that both fits your style and appeals to your audience.

When you think back on pitches that work, don't only rejoice in the win. Examine what made it successful. Determine which particular components had the greatest impact on your audience. Was there a particularly potent statistic that emphasised your point? An emotional tale from your own life? Revelry for a job well done offers a rich environment for improving your strategy.

Make use of this achievement as a model for future projects, examining what worked and making adjustments.

On the other hand, bad pitches might teach you valuable things. Don't be afraid to analyse these encounters. Rather, address them directly. Determine the errors in content, distribution, or engagement tactics. Maybe the images didn't support your story the way you planned, or maybe the time wasn't right. Openly acknowledge these qualities. This isn't about being stuck on the negative; rather, it's about realising where you need to make changes in order to improve.

Keep track of patterns on various pitches, even if they don't initially appear to be connected. Have you run into any comparable queries or objections? Identifying these similarities helps to form a stronger plan for future exchanges. Build a database of these encounters, connecting disparate pitches and shedding light on your future steps.

Stressing a growth-oriented mindset promotes resilience. Regardless of the result, every pitch is a foundation for future success.

Cultivating this mindset produces a culture where feedback and reflection are appreciated. Motivate your group to join you on this adventure, fostering a cooperative atmosphere centred on ongoing enhancement. Their observations, along with your own, paint a complete picture of your pitching ability.

Think about using technology to support your research. Making a pitch video might open your eyes in new ways. Observing oneself in action provides a fresh viewpoint on your body language, delivery, and engagement strategies. Because it shows you what the viewer sees, you can instantly improve the way you seem. Your learning curve can be accelerated by this objective viewpoint.

Establish a method for recording your analysis. It might be a digital platform or a spreadsheet that keeps track of your proposals and their results. Categorize each pitch by its merits, weaknesses, and audience reactions. It is simpler to look back on previous experiences with this structured method, seeing trends and patterns that inform your future growth.

Have role-playing games with your group. Practise possible pitches in a secure environment so you may try out various approaches. This exercise fosters spontaneity, which makes it easier for you to adjust to unforeseen enquiries or objections. It's an excellent method to get ready for a range of situations and increases your confidence in high-stakes situations.

Making connections with others in your industry can open up new ideas. Attend networking events, seminars, or workshops where pitching and stakeholder involvement are the topics of discussion. Peer exchanges can provide new perspectives and methods that were not previously thought of. Gaining knowledge from others quickens development and strengthens ties to the community.

Continuous Improvement-
Iterating Your Pitch

Pitch refinement is a dynamic process that changes with every presentation; it is not a one-time occurrence. Every interaction you have with potential stakeholders yields insightful information, and you can greatly increase your efficacy by being able to modify your message in response to feedback and changes in the business environment.

TO BEGIN WITH, ACKNOWLEDGE that the business environment is always changing. New technologies appear, customer preferences fluctuate, and market trends alter. It's crucial to keep up with these advancements, not just advantageous. A pitch that struck a chord yesterday might not do so the following day. This insight highlights the need for ongoing development.

Your greatest ally in this continuous process may be feedback. Actively solicit feedback from mentors, peers, and the audience following each pitch.

Establish a space where open communication is valued. "What did you like?" and "What actions could I have taken to improve?"are potent queries that open the door for helpful critique. Embrace this critique as an opportunity to refine your strategy.

Think about creating a formalised feedback system. After a presentation, send a brief survey to participants, asking them to offer their comments on various areas of your pitch. Clarity of the message, degree of involvement, and whether the suggested solution struck a chord are a few examples of possible questions. Being anonymous can motivate people to answer more honestly, which can let you see how you performed.

After you've gathered this information, carefully consider it. Seek for recurring themes and threads. Are there any particular areas where you get compliments or helpful criticism all the time? Finding these patterns will help you decide what to do next. Maybe your narrative strikes a chord, but the way the data is presented is boring.

A PITCH WILL BE MORE balanced and successful if it concentrates on strengthening areas that need improvement while keeping strengths.

Adapting your pitch to the ever-changing business environment is just as important as responding to criticism. Consumer expectations are changing, industries are changing, and markets are changing. Review the environment in which you work on a regular basis. Exist any cutting-edge technologies or trends that could improve your message?

By keeping yourself updated, you can modify your pitch to stay relevant and make sure you're always responding to your audience's wants and requirements right now.

Adaptability plays a significant part here. A good pitch must align with not only what you're selling but also with the current zeitgeist. Staying up to date with developments in your field is crucial. This could entail talking to thought leaders, reading reports from the sector, or going to conferences.

PARTICIPATING IN THESE discussions will deepen your comprehension and provide you the opportunity to incorporate these revelations into your presentations.

Additionally, think about experimenting with various pitch formats and styles. A fresh delivery can occasionally breathe new life into an otherwise boring presentation. This entails iterating and investigating other approaches rather than radically changing your strategy.

IF STORYTELLING HAS worked well for you in the past, think about combining graphics or interactive aspects. Or maybe you've had success with a data-driven strategy; think about how adding story components could improve that outcome.

Playing through scenarios as a team can also be an excellent way to test out new concepts. Exchange pitches with one another, experimenting with different tenors, tenors, and topics. This secure environment promotes original thinking and innovation.

As everyone on the team shares their ideas, you can come up with concepts that revolutionise your own pitch approach.

Examining previous proposals can also provide insightful insights. What functions well in one situation could spur novel ideas in another. Think about filming your presentations and watching them afterwards. Observing oneself can provide insightful insights into your body language, voice quality, and engagement techniques. Have there been times when you failed to hold the audience's interest?

Make changes based on these observations to improve your strategy for upcoming presentations.

While consistency is important, it doesn't mean stagnation. Making frequent revisions and changes to your pitch will guarantee that it changes with you and your audience. Your knowledge of what functions well and what doesn't will expand along with your business. This iterative process fosters a mindset that embraces change instead of being afraid of it.

BUILDING A PITCH MATERIAL library can also be a helpful resource. Create templates that allow you to swiftly alter your content for varied audiences. Slides, illustrations, handouts, and even one-pagers with important point summaries can be included in this library. Having a strong framework in place makes it easier to modify your pitch for various stakeholders, which will save you time without compromising the impact of your message.

THINK ABOUT THE STORYTELLING component of your proposal as well. Narratives establish relationships. They provide numbers and data a human face, enabling a deeper level of audience engagement with the subject.

Developing your narrative skills further can help your pitch have a stronger emotional effect. Examine fresh case studies or anecdotes that support your point of view. An ordinary pitch may become an unforgettable experience with the appropriate tale, creating a lasting impact on your audience.

Making connections in your field of expertise can also provide advice on how to pitch well. Talk to people who pitch their ideas all the time, whether they are investors, salespeople, or entrepreneurs. You can come up with fresh ideas for your own pitching techniques by talking about what works, learning from each other's experiences, and exchanging experiences.

SUMMARY

C ondensing the core of the journey you've travelled through each step of your pitching approach is more important than simply providing a summary of the main points of a pitch process. Imagine this as a colourful tapestry of experiences and insights that are woven together to tell a compelling story that appeals to stakeholders.

At the root of any good pitch lies preparation. Knowing your subject matter inside and out is crucial.

This entails being aware of your audience's demands and interests in addition to knowing your product or service. It is crucial to create an engaging narrative that links your solution to their objectives. Instead of approaching your pitch as a presentation, view it as a dialogue. Grab the attention of your audience right away by introducing them to interesting statistics or relatable anecdotes that relate to their experiences.

THE CRAFT OF STORYTELLING has great influence over how people see things. An engaging narrative draws listeners in, arouses feelings, and helps information stick in their minds. Your audience will be able to identify with your offering if you present your pitch as a story. This link turns inert data into understandable insights, elevating your idea from pertinent to crucial.

Being ready also means being ready for criticisms and queries. Understanding your audience entails being aware of any potential worries they may have.

Preemptively addressing these gives you the confidence to move the conversation in a positive way. Provide answers to potential roadblocks to bolster the importance of your idea and show that you have considered the intricacies involved.

The follow-up becomes an essential part of the process after the pitch. Requests for more information and thank-you notes keep things moving. These modest actions convey professionalism and gratitude.

They suggest that you're invested in the relationship, ready to engage further and address any lingering questions. Think of follow-up techniques to maintain the discussion. These touchpoints, which could include delivering progress reports, sharing pertinent articles, or offering more resources, support the relationship you've already started to establish.

Consistent communication is essential for building long-term partnerships with stakeholders.

Consistent updates regarding your enterprise, sector patterns, and accomplishments maintain your prominence. Establish a routine for your outreach—a monthly newsletter, for example, or a brief check-in. This not only informs your network but also demonstrates your dedication to openness and cooperation.

Following up with a pitch analysis enables introspection and development. Did the people in your audience react well? Was there ever a situation that you could have handled differently?

Gather feedback to spot trends and pinpoint areas that want work as well as those that have gone well. This process is an opportunity to grow, not to wallow in regret over past transgressions. Every encounter improves the one before it, helping you become more confident and hone your strategy.

Your pitch will always be better because you will have a dynamic mindset. Your communications should change along with the business environment. Keep up with changes in the market, emerging technology, and industry trends.

Make use of this information to modify your pitch so that it stays compelling and current. Here, experimentation is important. Try a variety of formats, stories, and visual aids to see what connects with your audience the most. You have the opportunity to improve your message and delivery with each iteration.

Networking inside your sector opens opportunities to fresh ideas and perspectives. Having conversations with mentors, colleagues, and possible investors expands your knowledge of successful pitching.

Attend conferences, join industry groups, and participate in conversations. These contacts generate inspiration and foster the exchange of best practices.

It is impossible to overestimate the importance of storytelling in your proposal. It offers a structure that makes difficult concepts easy to understand. Use vivid examples and relatable circumstances to explain the impact of your offering. As a result, the data becomes more than simply numbers and becomes a story that resonates with your audience.

People are more inclined to interact and become invested in your story when they can relate to it.

Perfecting your delivery is another aspect of crafting a pitch. Both the material and the method you portray it can have an impact. Be mindful of your tempo, vocal tone, and body language. When you're interested in the content, your confidence comes through. Practise until you can't make a mistake, not simply until you get it right. By practicing, you get more comfortable and can concentrate on making connections rather than memorising facts.

Peer and mentor feedback can be a great tool for improving your pitch. Ask dependable coworkers to attend your presentation. Their viewpoint has the power to highlight your message's weak points and offer fresh perspectives. This cooperative strategy fosters a culture of development, motivating all parties to advance their abilities.

The goal of cultivating relationships with stakeholders is to unite them around your vision. Every conversation fosters rapport and trust.

Genuineness is essential; honesty is valued more highly than well-preserved exteriors. Take a sincere interest in their opinions and requirements. In addition to fortifying relationships, this two-way communication opens the door for cooperation and support.

STRATEGIC ACTION PLAN FOR PITCHING YOUR BUSINESS

1. Define Your Objectives
   - Action Steps:
   - Identify what you want to achieve from your pitch (e.g., funding, partnerships, market entry).
   - Set measurable goals (e.g., securing three follow-up meetings within a month).

2. Know Your Audience

- Action Steps:

- Research the stakeholders who will be present at your pitch.

- Create profiles for each audience segment, including their interests, needs, and potential objections.

- Tailor your message to resonate with their priorities and expectations.

3. Craft Your Story
- Action Steps:

- Develop a compelling narrative that incorporates your business's mission and values.

- Use real-life examples and data to illustrate your points.

- Prepare a clear value proposition that explains how your offering meets the audience's needs.

4. PREPARE FOR OBJECTIONS
- Action Steps:

- Anticipate potential questions and objections from your audience.

- Develop clear, concise responses to address these concerns.

- Role-play with a trusted colleague to practice handling objections effectively.

5. Design Engaging Visuals
  - **Action Steps:**
  - Create visually appealing slides that complement your pitch.
  - Use charts, graphs, and images to enhance understanding and engagement.
  - Ensure that visuals support your narrative without overwhelming the audience.

6. REHEARSE YOUR DELIVERY
  - **Action Steps:**
  - Practice your pitch multiple times to build confidence.
  - Record yourself to evaluate your body language and vocal delivery.
  - Seek feedback from peers to refine your presentation style.

7. Follow-Up Strategy

- Action Steps:

- Prepare a template for thank-you notes to send after the pitch.

- Schedule reminders for follow-up communication based on stakeholder interest.

- Plan additional content to share, such as articles or updates related to your pitch.

8. Build Relationships
-Action Steps:

- Connect with stakeholders on professional networks like LinkedIn.

- Engage in regular communication, sharing relevant industry insights and updates.

- Organize informal meet-ups or virtual coffee chats to strengthen relationships over time.

9. ANALYZE FEEDBACK
- Action Steps:

- After each pitch, gather feedback from stakeholders and observers.

- Reflect on what worked well and what could be improved.

- Document lessons learned and apply them to future pitches.

10. Continuous Improvement

- Action Steps:

- Stay informed about industry trends and changes in the market landscape.
- Regularly review and update your pitch materials based on new insights.
- Set quarterly goals to refine your pitch and develop new strategies.

Don't miss out!

Visit the website below and you can sign up to receive emails whenever JOSHUA ZAGHE publishes a new book. There's no charge and no obligation.

https://books2read.com/r/B-A-BINQB-ZWACF

BOOKS 2 READ

Connecting independent readers to independent writers.

Did you love *How to Pitch Your Business: Proven Strategies to Stand Out and Win Over Stakeholders*? Then you should read *Never Talk Price to a Customer: How to Master the Art of Talking Value*[1] by JOSHUA ZAGHE!

Stop focusing on price. Customers don't care about numbers, they care about the value you offer. Picture yourself walking into a negotiation, not to haggle, but to show how your product or service improves their lives. When you shift the conversation from price to value, the cost becomes irrelevant. Customers won't ask for discounts if they see that what you're offering is truly valuable. They're not just buying a product; they're investing in solutions that improve their future.

Talking price limits you. When you lead with numbers, you get trapped in a race to the bottom, constantly compared with cheaper alternatives. But when you focus on value, you set yourself apart. You're not selling just a product anymore; you're offering results and experiences. Customers start asking how your solution will make their business, life, or future better. The conversation shifts to outcomes—what your product or service can do for them—and now,

1. https://books2read.com/u/m2a2oo

2. https://books2read.com/u/m2a2oo

you've sparked their interest. They become curious about the benefits and the transformation you're offering, and they stop caring about the price.

When customers feel the value, they don't question the price. The phrase "You get what you pay for" isn't about how much something costs, but about the outcome. The moment you get them to see beyond price tags, they start thinking, "How can this improve my life?" You want them to visualize how your product will solve their problems, remove their pain, and enhance their lives. They'll imagine their future with your solution, and desire will build. That emotional connection is what turns consideration into a need. You're no longer discussing costs—you're selling a vision of success that your product delivers.

Guide your customer through this vision. Don't just talk about features—show them the results they'll get with your solution. Make them feel the potential. When you talk value, customers view your product as an investment, not an expense. They'll be ready to buy, knowing that what they're getting isn't just a product but a transformative tool. The price? That becomes secondary. Once you've shown them the immense value, they won't look at competitors, they won't seek cheaper alternatives. They'll be sold, ready to act on the undeniable benefits you've outlined, and that's where the sale happens—because value always outweighs the price.

Also by JOSHUA ZAGHE

Milton Keynes UK
Ingram Content Group UK Ltd.
UKHW032031191024
449814UK00010B/620

9 798227 331977